A PROMISE
TO OUR
COUNTRY

by Captain Jam

pictures by Jam

WHITTLESEY HOUSE
McGraw-Hill Book Company, Inc.
New York   Toronto   London

Copyright © 1961 by James Calvert and James Daugherty
All rights reserved.
Library of Congress Catalog Card Number: 61-9468
Published by Whittlesey House,
a division of the McGraw-Hill Book Company, Inc.
Printed in the United States of America.

A PROMISE TO OUR COUNTRY

"I pledge allegiance..."

Calvert, USN

Daugherty

Every morning, in almost every schoolhouse of this great country, a very important promise is made. It is made by you. It is made by boys and girls who live in Maine. It is made by boys and girls in California. From the territory of Puerto Rico to our newest state, Hawaii, children start the day with a promise.

What promise?
You make it when you say:

I PLEDGE ALLEGIANCE TO THE FLAG OF THE UNITED
STATES OF AMERICA AND TO THE REPUBLIC FOR WHICH
IT STANDS, ONE NATION, UNDER GOD, INDIVISIBLE,
WITH LIBERTY AND JUSTICE FOR ALL.

Why is this pledge so important?

5

What does it really mean?   What do we mean when we say:

"I PLEDGE ALLEGIANCE . . ."

A pledge is a promise. When we pledge our allegiance,
we promise to be faithful.

". . . TO THE FLAG OF THE
                UNITED STATES OF AMERICA . . ."

All over the world, our flag stands
for the United States of America.

You know what our flag looks like. But do you know
what the colors, the stars, and the stripes all stand for?
Our first president, George Washington, explained
the meanings of the colors for us. Remembering
the red of the English flag, he said: "We take the star
from Heaven, the red from our mother country,
separating it by white stripes to show that
we have separated from her . . ."

Today when we talk about the Red, White, and Blue everyone knows we mean the American flag.

The background of seven red stripes and six white stripes stands for the thirteen original colonies. It does not change. The number of stars, however, does change. When our flag was new there were only thirteen stars in the blue field—one for each of the colonies. However, each time we add a new state to our country we add a new star to our flag.

For almost fifty years we had forty-eight states in our country and forty-eight stars in our flag. But in 1959 we added a new star for Alaska and then, in 1960, another new one for Hawaii, the fiftieth state.

But a flag is still just a piece of cloth. Why should we promise to be faithful to a piece of colored cloth?

Just as a promise is important because of what it stands for, this piece of red, white, and blue cloth we call our flag is important because it stands for something.

In our pledge, we promise faithfulness to the flag

"... AND TO THE REPUBLIC
FOR WHICH IT STANDS ..."

When we say our country is a republic, we are
talking about the kind of government we have. In a
republic, all the people vote. They vote for men to represent
them in the government. The men the people elect
are called senators and representatives. These senators
and representatives are responsible to the people that elected
them. They must make laws that will do the best for
the people they represent.

Abraham Lincoln, our sixteenth president, in one of his greatest speeches, gave a description of our government, when he said it was ". . . of the people, by the people, and, for the people . . ."

The men who run our government are some *of* the people who are elected *by* the rest of the people to govern in a way that is best *for* all the people.

When you are grown up, you will be able to vote
as your mother and father do now. Your vote will give
you a chance to have your share in running the government.
Who knows, perhaps someday, because we live in a
republic, people may be casting their votes for you.
A vote is a valuable and important thing.

". . . ONE NATION . . ."

Our nation is made up of fifty states but we all belong to one nation. We are like a big family of fifty brothers and sisters.

A very big family indeed! Starting with the lakes and forests of Maine and reaching to Hawaii in the middle of the Pacific Ocean, our country stretches almost a fourth of the way around the earth. But even though we are so large, and divided into fifty different parts, the most important thing about us is that we are one nation.

For over 150 years our coins have had a motto
on them—E PLURIBUS UNUM. If you have a penny,
you can find this motto. It is written in Latin and means
"Out of many, one" or "out of many states, one nation."

Before the American colonists won their independence in
the Revolutionary War, our first thirteen states were thirteen
separate little colonies. These thirteen colonies decided to join
together into one nation, a republic called the United States.

However, it was not as easy for the new family of states to get along together as some had hoped.
Each of the thirteen states wanted to make the rules for the new country. They did not want another state telling them what they could or could not do.

The founding fathers settled all this by writing down rules for the entire country in a long paper called the Constitution. It allowed each state to make the rules (or laws) about things that just concerned itself. But the rules that applied to the whole country had to be made by everyone.

The Constitution was very wisely written and, even today, it is the basis on which our democracy is run. It is largely because our founding fathers wrote such a good set of original laws that our family of states has been able to remain together as one nation.

"... UNDER GOD ..."

These words were not in our pledge when it was first written. They were added by an act of Congress in 1954. When our thirty-fourth president, Dwight D. Eisenhower, signed the act to make it a law, he said this change to our pledge would remind us of the importance that a firm belief in God has always played in the history of our nation.

It is interesting that Francis Scott Key, the man who wrote our national anthem, "The Star-Spangled Banner," said: "And let this be our motto: In God is our trust."

". . . INDIVISIBLE . . ."

When we say our nation is indivisible we mean that it cannot be split up into a group of little countries.

You remember how important our founding fathers thought it was for us to be the United States—you remember how they wrote our Constitution with this purpose especially in mind.

Well, like all families, we have had our arguments. Most of these arguments we have been able to settle by talking them out or by voting.

However, one argument came very close to dividing us. About one hundred years ago the northern and southern states had a terrible series of arguments about things they both felt were important.

A war between the northern and the southern
states was the result. It was the only war we
have ever fought between states—it was a bloody
and awful war, but it did not divide the country.

In fact, terrible as it was, the war served the purpose of making us realize the importance of remaining united, just as an argument in a family can make its members realize how important the family and its love are to them.

". . . WITH LIBERTY . . ."

At the entrance to New York Harbor is the statue of a lady holding a torch high in the air. When ships from all over the world enter New York Harbor, they look for the Statue of Liberty; the statue is the symbol of our country to men who cross the ocean to find it.

The statue stands for liberty, perhaps the most important word in America.

Our Declaration of Independence,
our Constitution, our laws, and the men
who run our government, are all
dedicated to keeping the United States
a land of liberty—a land
where people can come and go
as they please and say what they
believe, so long as they do not
harm anyone by their actions.

In 1941, our thirty-second president, Franklin D. Roosevelt, told us that liberty should mean four freedoms:

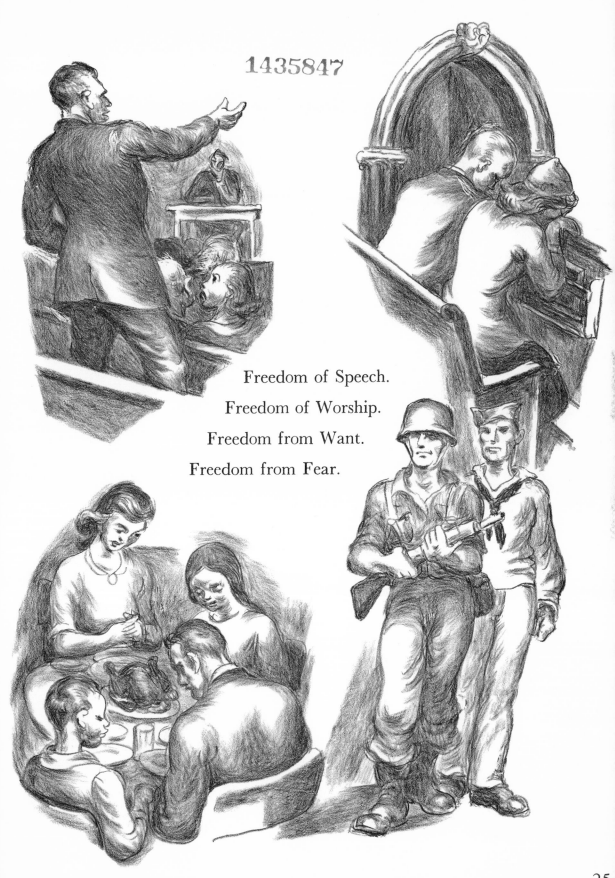

1435847

Freedom of Speech.

Freedom of Worship.

Freedom from Want.

Freedom from Fear.

". . . AND JUSTICE FOR ALL."

We have seen that our nation, like our school and
like our family, must have rules, or laws, to make it work.

When we talk about justice we are talking about the way in which these rules are carried out. When everyone is treated the same way according to the rules in existence, then we say that justice is being done.

Our Constitution promises equal and fair treatment for all—regardless of their race or what they believe—regardless of whether they are rich or poor, old or young. This is what we mean by justice—the same rules and the same privileges for everyone.

The Pledge of Allegiance is usually recited, but it can also be sung.

PLEDGE OF ALLEGIANCE TO THE FLAG

Musical Setting by
IRVING CAESAR – ASCAP

March Time
Intro.

VOICE

I pledge al - le-giance, pledge al - le-giance, Pledge al - le-giance to the flag, To the

flag of the U - nit - ed States of A - mer-i - ca, A - mer-i - ca, And

to the Re - pub - lic for which it stands!

CHORUS

One Na-tion un-der God, One Na-tion un-der God, In-di-vis-i-ble with lib-er-ty and jus-tice for all, In-di-vis-i-ble with lib-er-ty and jus-tice for all. One jus - tice for all.

rit. - al - Fine

vbrs.

29

When our founding fathers wrote the Declaration of Independence they wrote a pledge at the end of it. They said that for the support of the Declaration, ". . . we mutually pledge to each other our Lives, our Fortunes and our sacred Honor."

These men and women kept that promise and the new nation they founded grew into the finest and most wonderful the world has ever known.

Now it is our responsibility to protect, work for, and help make better, this wonderful nation of ours.

Each of us has a sacred trust of his own concerning the future of this country. John F. Kennedy, our thirty-fifth President, expressed this for us when he said:

"The next year, the next decade, in all likelihood the next generation, will require more bravery and wisdom on our part than any period in our history."

And that is what we are promising when we pledge allegiance to the flag each morning. We are promising to do our best to keep this greatest of all nations strong and free; indivisible, with liberty and justice for all.

THE HISTORY OF OUR PLEDGE

Our pledge was written by Francis Bellamy, who was born at Mount Morris, New York, on May 18, 1855, and died August 28, 1931.   He wrote it for a very special event: the dedication of the World's Fair Grounds in Chicago. The dedication took place on Columbus Day, October 21, 1892, the four hundredth anniversary of the discovery of America.

The original pledge was changed slightly by the First and Second Flag Conferences in 1923 and 1924.   On December 28, 1945, the Congress of the United States officially declared it to be the "Pledge of Allegiance to the Flag."

On Flag Day, June 14, 1954, President Dwight D. Eisenhower signed the law which added the words "under God."

The Song "Pledge of Allegiance to the Flag" was written by Irving Caesar.   On Flag Day, June 14, 1955, it was sung for the first time, by the official Air Force choral group in special Flag Day ceremonies in the House of Representatives.

ABOUT THE AUTHOR AND ARTIST

CAPTAIN JAMES CALVERT is Commander of Submarine Division 102, which contains all of the nuclear submarines in our country's Atlantic Fleet. Before this, he was Commanding Officer of the USS *Skate,* the nuclear submarine which made two voyages to the North Pole. He tells about these trips in his book for grown-ups, *Surface at the Pole.* But all of Captain Calvert's time is not spent with submarines! He spends many pleasant off-duty hours at home in Mystic, Connecticut, with his wife and three children.

JAMES DAUGHERTY is the nationally known and well-loved artist. He has illustrated over 100 children's books, and has used his talents in other branches of art, such as mural painting.

Mr. Daugherty has also written some of the books that he has illustrated. Among them are *Andy and the Lion* and *Poor Richard.* In 1940, his book *Daniel Boone* was awarded the Newbery Award by the American Library Association for "the most distinguished contribution to children's literature" that year. Mr. Daugherty and his wife live in Westport, Connecticut. They have one son who is also an author and artist.